POWER

OVER

POPULARITY

Ayannah Williams

ACKNOWLEDGEMENTS

Years ago, I would have never imagined that I would be a published author for the Kingdom of GOD. Yet, here I am today with book #3. All I can say is, "Wow GOD, You did it!". I give GOD honor, praise and glory for the gifts that He has placed on the inside of me, and I thank Him so much for saving me and filling me with the Holy Ghost.

A loving thank you to my mom and dad who have been very supportive of my ministry. Thank you both so much for your prayers and encouragement. I am the woman I am today because of the both of you. I love you.

To my family, friends and those who continually support me and encourage me to be the best Ayannah that I can be, Thank You. Your

FOREWORD

By: Yolanda Adams
Award Winning Gospel Recording Artist,
Producer and Media Owner

I have been privileged to know Lady Ayannah since she was a little girl. We all knew that GOD had something special for her to do, but we did not know that aside from her musical talents, she would be a powerfully anointed force of GOD! This book will give you a refreshing look at keeping your focus and pressing forward. Read it and be enlightened.

TABLE OF CONTENTS

Prayer of Salvation 9

Introduction 13

Chapter 1: "Quench Not the Spirit" 21

Chapter 2: "Spiritual Wickedness in High
Places" 33

Chapter 3: "A Form of godliness" 39

Chapter 4: "Be Filled with the Holy Ghost" 45

Chapter 5: "Suffering, Persecution and
Rejection" 51

Chapter 6: "Ye Shall Receive Power" 65

Chapter 7: "Wake Up" 83

"Salvation- A Free Gift"

Scripture: "That if thou shalt confess with thy mouth the Lord Jesus, and shalt believe in thine heart that God hath raised him from the dead, thou shalt be saved. For with the heart man believeth unto righteousness; and with the mouth confession is made unto salvation."

Romans 10:9-10

"Repent, and be baptized every one of you in the name of Jesus Christ for the remission of sins, and ye shall receive the gift of the Holy Ghost."

Acts 2:38

Are you saved? If you died at this moment, are you confident that you would spend eternity with Christ? If you are not sure, then TODAY is your day! The most important decision you will ever make in your life is to give your life to Jesus Christ. The whole purpose of our earthly existence is to be in fellowship with God. He desires a close relationship with YOU. Jesus died so that you could live a life free from the bondage of sin and death. When you accept Jesus into your heart, you receive a new beginning, a fresh start and a brand new way of living. All you have to do is believe! Are you ready to receive Christ now? Say this prayer out loud as your confession that you believe.

Prayer of Salvation

Dear Jesus, I believe You are the Son of God. I believe You died for me on the cross and shed Your innocent blood for my sins. I believe that God raised You from the dead on the third day and You are now seated at the right hand of the Father. I recognize that I am a sinner and I repent of my sins. Please forgive my sins and wash me with Your blood. Come into my heart. Save my soul as I give my life to You. I make You my Lord and Savior. Fill me with Your Spirit. I will now live the rest of my life for You. I am born again. In the name of Jesus, Amen.

You did it! You are saved! The Bible declares that when one sinner repents, angels rejoice! Second Corinthians 5:17 states, "Therefore if any man be in Christ, he is a new creature: old things are passed away; behold, all things become new."

You are brand new! Welcome to the Kingdom of GOD!

"Power Over Popularity"

"...These that have turned the world upside down..."

Acts 17:6

Introduction

1 Corinthians 4:20 "For the kingdom of God is not in word, but in power."

I am convinced that many believers are currently on spiritual life support, looking for something more; searching for something that would quench their soul's desires. Thirsting and hungering for more of GOD. More than a Sunday service, more than a prayer meeting, more than a women's day program and more than a family and friends day. In actuality, what we are searching for is not another word from GOD, but we are in need of a true, authentic move of GOD. 1 Corinthians 4:20 declares, "For the kingdom of God is not in word, but in power." We are searching for manifestation and demonstration; an encounter with the most Holy One. And while we are seeking and searching for more of GOD, GOD is seeking and searching for someone that He can manifest His power through. I hear the scripture saying, "Whom shall I send, and who will go for us?"

(Isaiah 6:8). GOD says, "Are you the one, or should He look for another?" Where are the people that want GOD for real? Where are the individuals that will give up everything that this life has to offer and be the sacrifice? Who can GOD trust to carry His glory? Where are the Elijah's? Where are the apostles? Where are the true prophets? GOD says, "Come out of your hiding caves", for He is about to use you to slew Jezebel. Where are the David's chasing after GOD's own heart? Who wants it for real? Who wants GOD's power to rest on their life? Where are the ones that could care less about being popular; and the ones who could care less about being liked and accepted? Who will stand up and fight Goliath? Who is willing to go against the spirit of tradition and carry a real move of GOD? Where are you? In this season, it's Power over Popularity.

I believe personally that the writer of the book of Ecclesiastes, the son of David, had an experience one day where he sat back and observed certain areas in life and realized, all of the things that we care so much about are meaningless. The things that we put so much emphasis on are vain. Comparably, one day I did a similar assessment of life, and I found his observations to be true. In my life, I have perceived this one aspect to be solid, only what you do for Christ will last. Wholeheartedly, I have devoted my life to the Kingdom of GOD in whatever shape, form or fashion that GOD needs me. Because of this, I have submitted to the will of GOD for my life and not what I wanted or desired. In essence, this means that I had to remove myself from some places, distance myself from some people and lean on GOD when I had nothing else. It was in my times of testing and my trials of fire that I learned who GOD was. I did not run away from the trials, but I submitted to them. It was in my trials that I gained a strength in GOD that came with the power of GOD on my life.

Isaiah 43:2 (NIV) says, "When you pass through the waters, I will be with you; and when you pass through the rivers, they will not sweep over you. When you walk through the fire, you will not be burned; the flames will not set you ablaze." It is interesting that this verse mentions three natural elements (waters, rivers and fire) that have the potential to consume you and destroy you. Yet, GOD says in this verse, "when you pass through" and "when you walk through", these elements will not have any effect on you. By GOD using the terms "pass through" and "walk through", it is a clear indication that this is a process you will have to "go through". But when you come out, (glory to GOD, I feel the Holy Ghost), you will not be same. Here is why...the natural elements that GOD used in this scripture essentially have supernatural meanings. Let's take a look at the first element: water. Water represents the cleansing power of the Blood of Jesus. When you receive Christ in your life as your personal Savior, the Blood of Jesus cleanses you from all of your sins. Now, look at the second element: rivers. Rivers are metaphoric examples of the infilling of the Holy Ghost. After you have been saved by grace and cleansed with the Blood of Jesus, GOD then fills you with His Holy Spirit. Jesus declares in John 7:38, "He that believeth on me, as the scripture hath said, out of his belly shall flow rivers of living water." The third element mentioned in Isaiah 43:2 is fire. The "fire" comes to purge your life and consume anything in your flesh that is not like GOD. The "fire" sent in your life purges out unrighteousness and creates space for the fire of GOD to sit on your life. It is the fire of GOD that makes you powerful. Let us take a look at another scripture. Luke 3:16, "John answered, saying unto *them* all, I indeed baptize you with water; but one mightier than I cometh, the latchet of whose shoes I am not worthy to unloose: he shall baptize you with the Holy Ghost and with fire." Did you catch that? The same three elements from Isaiah 43:2, "water, the Holy Ghost (rivers) and fire", were also mentioned in Luke 3:16. In conclusion, you must be saved and you must be filled with the Holy Ghost in order for the fire and power of GOD to rest on your life.

CHAPTER 1:

"Quench Not the Spirit"

Amos 6:1 "Woe to them that are at ease in Zion..." As I began writing this book, one of the first words I heard in my spirit was "complacency". According to Webster's dictionary, complacency is defined as, "self-satisfaction with an existing situation and/or condition." The spirit of complacency is the spirit that says, "That will do", "This is good enough" or "I am ok with where I am. I'm satisfied"; but in the name of Jesus, I slaughter that spirit of complacency in the body of Christ. Woe to you who are at ease in Zion. There should never come a place in your life where you are satisfied with where you are in GOD. Each day you should be growing and striving in the things of the Lord. Though I have seen powerful and notable moves of GOD within my ministry, I am not satisfied until the dead are raised, the sick are healed, the lame walk, the deaf hear, the blind see, the tormented are free and sinners are saved. Though Jesus promised that greater works we shall do, there must be a personal and continual strive towards those greater works. Paul stated in Philippians 3:12-14, "Not as though I had already attained, either were already perfect: but I follow after, if that I may apprehend that for which also I am apprehended of Christ Jesus. Brethren, I count not myself to have apprehended: but this one thing I do, forgetting those things which are behind, and reaching forth unto those things which are before, I "press" (STRIVE) toward the mark of the prize of the high calling of God in Christ Jesus". Paul is stating that despite all of the great things he has seen GOD do through him and in him, he has still not yet reached or attained his goal, nor has he been perfected in the things of GOD. Nevertheless, he forgets what is behind him and he continues to press forward. Meaning, there is more to GOD than what you have seen. There is more to GOD than what you have experienced. There are greater levels in GOD than where you are. Do not become complacent. Keep striving in the things of the Lord.

Before I continue with the rest of my book, I would like to start by saying that what I am about to say does not apply to every leader or every church. This book may not even apply to you. However, within my years of being in ministry, I have noticed many things along the way. One day I had a conversation with an older lady at lunch and she expressed to me her love for GOD and how good GOD had been to her. However, in the midst of our conversation, she said, "I've been at the same church for over 20 years, and for over 20 years, we have been doing the same thing." I was floored. She expressed how she had begun to desire

more of GOD. Her hunger and thirst for GOD had
begun to grow, but she was not being fulfilled
within her church. One day she said she prayed and
asked GOD what she should do, and He responded
by telling her that the gate was closing and that she
was released from that church. In other words, the
brook had dried up. In 1 Kings Chapter 17, the
Lord told Elijah to hide himself by the brook and to
drink from the brook while the ravens fed him.
Elijah did as commanded for a period of time, but
in verse 7, the Bible states that the brook dried up
because there had been no rain. That is when the
word of the Lord came to Elijah commanding him
to get up and go to Zarephath. What am I saying?
In order for a plant to grow, it has to be in an
environment conducive for growth. Essentially, in
order for you to grow spiritually, you have to been
in an environment that is conducive for your

growth. You cannot expect a flower to grow in a desert. You have to move as GOD commands you.

I have preached in many churches, and I have noticed that even when GOD is trying to move by shifting and doing something new, the mindset of the people restricts GOD from moving due to traditional customs and views. Tradition says, "It has to be done this way and no other way because this is the way we have done it for years". The problem with that is, when GOD gets ready to do a new thing, we are restricted by the use of traditional, antiquated and outdated methods and ways of doing things. This keeps people stagnated and hinders their faith from ever growing with expectancy to see GOD in a new way. I have been in atmospheres where the Spirit of GOD was moving powerfully, yet because of traditional mindsets and even individuals lack of reverencing the presence and move of GOD, they would shift the atmosphere by playing a fast paced, up-tempo song. Inevitably, this killed the atmosphere and hindered the move of GOD. This is what the Bible is speaking of in 1 Thessalonians 5:19 when it says, "Quench not the Spirit". If the Bible tells us not to do it, and then we do it, that is sin. What does the word "quench" mean? One definition is, "to put out or extinguish". Now, take a look at the word "extinguish". In most cases, we use the word "extinguish" when we are referring to a fire. Hebrews 12:29 states, "For our God is a consuming fire". So what GOD is ultimately saying in 1 Thessalonians 5:19 is, "Do not be found guilty of putting out My fire". When GOD is moving in a service, at the gas station, at the grocery store or on a basketball court, LET HIM.

Think about this, every year Apple releases a

new phone or gadget to keep up with the ever changing times and technology demands. Yet within our spiritual economic systems and institutions, we are YEARS behind, refusing to change; refusing to try new things to accommodate what GOD is doing. We have become comfortable with hardly anyone getting saved in our Sunday services, just as long as we can say we had church. Our sole purpose for doing ministry should be to see lost souls come to Christ. When we begin to focus on who has the biggest church, who has the most members, or who is doing more in the community, then we have lost focus. The body of Christ is not in competition, we are in conjunction. 1 Corinthians 12:12 "For as the body is one, and hath many members, and all the members of that one body, being many, are one body: so also is Christ." It is time that we join forces together, shift with what GOD is doing and go completely after the lost.

Part of the church's design was to be a place of spiritual education, almost like a college. In essence, people come in, they learn, they grow and then they proceed to the next level and dimension. Which means, not everyone within a church will stay at that church forever. Based on their spiritual grade level and assignment in the Body of Christ, GOD may cause them to shift and even shift out to accommodate their assignment. When a person leaves a church based on their assignment within that season, it is never intended to make any church or leader look unqualified or insufficient. It is just an indication that that person has gained everything that they needed from that particular spiritual institution and GOD has graduated them to the next level.

In certain circumstances, however, I have noticed that instead of spiritual institutions being a place of healing and preparation for individuals to be sent out to preach the gospel and win the lost, it has become a place of bondage. One day while I was ministering, the Spirit of the Lord spoke to me and said, "I have an ought with the church." He said, "The church was never designed to keep you bound." In other words, the place where we were supposed to be free, has become the place where we are bound. Bound by fear; afraid to attend and visit other churches for the edifying of your spirit. Bound by control; Leaders using manipulation as a tool to keep you under their control and submission. So in reality, what GOD was saying was, we are locked in the church, ministering to one another, getting fat in the spirit, afraid to step out and be who GOD has called us to be, while the people in our communities and in the world are out there lost and dying. The honest truth is that most people who need GOD are not coming to church. I believe in my heart this is the exact reason why Jesus told the disciples to "GO" into all the world and preach the gospel to every creature. He commanded the disciples to be fishermen of men. It is time for the church to get on a move. Come outside of the four walls of the church and meet people where they are. Now, while this book may not be for everybody, there is somebody who is going to read this and be empowered to seek GOD, live holy, and pursue Holy Ghost power in order to win souls for the Kingdom of GOD. Is it you?

CHAPTER 2:

"Spiritual Wickedness in High Places"

One night I had a dream where I was preaching to a group of people in a small setting. In the dream, as I was ministering powerfully under the influence of the Holy Ghost, I began to tell the people, "The problem is, you are sitting under leaders who aren't working with any more power than you are. Because of this, these same leaders have become jealous of you". Then the dream ended. It was the same scenario that happened to David when he was under Saul's leadership. Saul was still holding the position as King even though GOD had rejected him. And though Saul held the position, in the eyes of GOD, he was fired. As a result, GOD took His Spirit away from Saul and placed it upon David. The Bible makes it clear that Saul "saw" that the LORD was with David. Because of this, Saul began to fear David and became envious of him. What really caused Saul to have a jealous spirit? In 1 Samuel Chapter 18, there was a celebration taking place for King Saul. The Bible says that the women came out to meet King Saul with singing and dancing, with joy and musical instruments. Yet, in the midst of the celebration, the women began to praise David and exalt David higher than Saul. 1 Samuel 18:7, the women said, "Saul has slain his thousands, and David his ten thousands." It was not that Saul did not know what David was capable of. In actuality, it was Saul who had set David over the men of war because of how successful David was in every battle. Saul put David in that position. Yet, this was the same Saul who became envious of the leader he had put in charge. The problem was not that David had great accomplishments, the problem was that the people began to praise David in Saul's house. In other words, they were not praising the bishop or the pastor, but they were praising the little minister sitting on the back pew full of the Holy Ghost. David carried a real anointing because the Lord was with him. Because of this, Saul was jealous.

One day the Spirit of the Lord began to speak to me, and He said that He was getting ready to expose the hearts and motives of leaders and it would shock a lot of people. Witchcraft in pulpits; spirits of manipulation; the control of others through mind games and domination; using God-given authority as a form of control; boxing in, shutting up, sitting down, and closing off people that GOD has anointed in this season to do great works for the Kingdom. Ephesians 6:12, "For we wrestle not against flesh and blood, but against principalities, against powers, against the rulers of the darkness of this world, against SPIRITUAL WICKEDNESS IN HIGH PLACES". The LORD spoke to me by way of revelation that when the scripture says "spiritual wickedness in high places", it is referring to leaders who hold high positions in our spiritual institutions but are under the influence of demonic spirits; controlling people through pulpits, manipulation and mind games. Witchcraft is not always magic and spells. Witchcraft is saying, "If you leave my church, you won't succeed".

CHAPTER 3:

"A Form of godliness"

"In the last days perilous times shall come. For men shall be lovers of their own selves, covetous, boasters, proud, blasphemers, disobedient to parents, unthankful, unholy, without natural affection, trucebreakers, false accusers, incontinent, fierce, despisers of those that are good, traitors, heady, high-minded, lovers of pleasures more than lovers of God; Having a form of godliness, but denying the power thereof: from such turn away."

2 Timothy 3: 1-5

"...having a form of godliness, but denying the power thereof". This is the spirit that wears the mask of holiness but lives unholy; shouts all around the church but openly living in sin, operating under the influence of a familiar spirit, living a double life. This same spirit preaches a good message but with no power; believes in Jesus only to an extent, but not enough to allow the conviction of the Holy Ghost to operate in their lives. It desires the nice church, the large congregation and the spotlight, but does not desire holiness and does not believe in the operation and the power of the Holy Ghost. Jesus said in Matthew 15:8 (NIV), "These people honor me with their lips, but their hearts are far from me". I have seen many operating in mass church, but not operating in mass deliverance, salvation and demonstration. Big does not mean powerful. In this season, GOD is shifting things. He is about to raise up a people that will and can demonstrate His power. No more of God's people, whether saint or sinner, coming in one way and leaving out the same. He is getting ready to show forth His Glory. He is about to separate the wheat from the tare, the real from the fake, the holy from the unholy, the clean from the unclean, the thief from the giver, the pure hearted leaders from the abusers. He is getting ready to expose it. GOD said, "In this season you either want power or you want popularity. You either want My Spirit, or you don't." Just because a person is in the church does not make them godly. GOD says there is a shift getting ready to take place in the body of Christ. The people that you once looked up to, GOD said He is getting ready to bring them down. WHY? Because they refuse obey Him. Married pastors that are sleeping with other women; leaders lusting after people in their congregation; perverted worship leaders who have not been delivered but are leading service. GOD says, "I am getting ready to expose it". There have been warnings after warnings, and still no change. What fellowship does light have with darkness? This is the exact reason why most of the world sees the church as a joke. People who profess to be Christians are living just as foul as those in the world. You can hardly distinguish between the saint and the sinner. This is what is called "having a form of godliness". GOD said He is sick of it. When are you going to get sick of your sin? When will you come to a place where you are tired of yourself? When you get to that place, that is when GOD can deliver you. However, there is a generation of believers who will obey and who will stand up for holiness. There is a generation of those who will not misrepresent the Kingdom of GOD. There is a generation that have made up their minds that they will live for GOD wholeheartedly. These are the generation of people that GOD is raising up. "And all the trees of the field shall know that I the LORD have brought down the high tree, have exalted the low tree, have dried up the green tree, and have made the dry tree to flourish: I the LORD have spoken and have done it" Ezekiel 17:24.

CHAPTER 4:

"Be Filled with the Holy Ghost"

The truth is, receiving the free gift of Salvation is inevitably the best decision that you will ever make in your lifetime. However, you need to be filled with God's Spirit. It is being filled with the Holy Ghost that helps you to live a holy life pleasing unto GOD. Not only that, but also the Holy Ghost is our Teacher and our Comforter. He leads and guides us into all truth. He teaches us of the things of GOD, and He convicts us in our errors. Before you embark upon completing the assignment and task that GOD has for you, it is important to be clothed with power from GOD. In Acts Chapter 1, Jesus told the disciples not to leave Jerusalem but to wait for the promise of the Father which was the baptism of the Holy Ghost. Ten days later, when the day of Pentecost had fully come, they were all filled with the Holy Ghost and began to speak in tongues.

In Acts 19, Paul encountered several believers in Ephesus, and he asked them a very profound question. Paul said unto them in verse two, "Have ye received the Holy Ghost since ye believed?" They replied unto him, "We have not so much as heard whether there be any Holy Ghost." This is quite interesting because it shows that being a believer is only one dimension of the faith. However, being filled with the Holy Ghost takes you into another dimension in GOD. As a believer, you must be filled with the Holy Ghost. It was after these men were baptized in the name of Jesus that Paul laid his hands on them and the Holy Ghost came on them (verse 6). It was then that these believers spoke with tongues and prophesied.

If you want to see your life and ministry go to the next dimension of power, you need to seek the infilling of the Holy Ghost. The infilling of the

Holy Ghost causes a fearlessness to come upon you to be able to speak the Word of GOD with boldness. Acts 4:31 says, "And when they had prayed, the place was shaken where they were assembled together; and they were all filled with the Holy Ghost, and they spake the word of God with boldness." In our walk with GOD, GOD desires us to be bold. Proverbs 28:1 "The righteous are as bold as a lion".

The infilling of the Holy Ghost also grants you wisdom. Wisdom is necessary to know how to, what to, when to and when not to. "Stephen, full of faith and power, did great wonders and miracles among the people. Then there arose certain of the synagogue, which is called the synagogue of the Libertines, and Cyrenians, and Alexandrians, and of them of Cilicia and of Asia, disputing with Stephen. And they were not able to resist the wisdom and the spirit by which he spake" (Acts 6:8-10). When you have the infilling of the Holy Ghost, those who dispute with you will not be able to resist the wisdom by which you speak. And GOD is so gracious that the scripture tells us in James 1:5 (NLT), "If you need wisdom, ask our generous God, and he will give it to you. He will not rebuke you for asking". GOD has no problem with granting wisdom to those who ask.

Here is something that I find interesting. In Acts 5:32, Peter explains that the Holy Ghost is given by GOD to those who obey Him. Did you realize that? GOD gives the Holy Ghost to them that obey. There is a level of obedience that GOD seeks from you as you seek His Spirit. GOD is getting ready to raise you up like never before, but GOD says there is an instruction, "You MUST obey". It is your obedience that outweighs your sacrifices. Your obedience outweighs your fasting. Obedience outweighs your daily Bible reading. It far exceeds your prayer life. GOD says, "Obedience is what I'm looking for". Will you obey?

CHAPTER 5:

"Suffering, Persecution and Rejection"

Power over Popularity - The truth about being powerful in GOD is that you will not be popular with people. You will not be liked or accepted by those who are intimidated by what you carry. People will look at you and count you out. On the contrary, GOD does not look at the outer appearance. The Bible indicates that He looks at the heart. 1 Samuel 16:7, "For the Lord seeth not as man seeth; for man looketh on the outward appearance, but the Lord looketh on the heart". Because of all that I have seen and experienced within different atmospheres, it drove me to a place where I said, "I'd rather have power than have popularity. I'd rather people hate me, but be confident that when I lay hands on the sick, they recover. I would rather people talk about me, but I know that when I cast a demon out, he has to obey. You can scandalize my name, but I am confident that demons recognize who I am and my authority in Christ". Power over Popularity! GOD says, "I am raising up a generation that does not want the popularity, neither do they want the big church, the prestige or the money, but what they want is to help save those that are lost."

Suffering

When you desire to be powerful in GOD, persecution and suffering must come. It inevitably comes right before you are about to be elevated and promoted in the things of GOD. Consider Joseph, thrown into a pit by his brothers, sold into slavery, accused by Potiphar's wife and thrown into prison. All of these incidents took place in his life as GOD was preparing to elevate and promote him as the Ruler of Egypt. Think about David. Before GOD made him the King of Israel, David spent years running from Saul. Now, consider Job. Job suffered a tremendous amount of suffering and loss, yet GOD restored Job with double. Suffering produces a level of obedience that is needed to please GOD as we live our daily lives. Hebrews 5:8 states that Jesus learned obedience through the things He suffered. David proclaims in Psalm 119:71, "It is good for me that I have been afflicted: that I might learn thy statutes." Suffering and affliction produce a humbleness in your spirit. There is no room for pride when your spirit is crushed. Understand that what causes you to be powerful in GOD is not how many scriptures you can quote. The power comes when you have been beaten down to nothing and you have been stripped of everything. Then GOD says, "Now I can use you." "Now I can pour my Spirit into you". Your experiences make you powerful. When you have experienced everything but death itself, you are able to help so many people with your testimonies. Romans 8:18 declares, "For I reckon that the sufferings of this present time are not worthy to be compared with the glory which shall be revealed in us." Allow the things that you have suffered and will suffer to empower you.

Persecution

When you have devoted your life and ministry to GOD, you should automatically expect persecution. 2 Timothy 3:12 tells us, "All that will live godly in Christ Jesus shall suffer persecution". Persecution must come. Ironically, I am appalled to say that majority of the persecution I have faced in my life and ministry came from those within the body of Christ. It is expected that the people of the world would hate us. Jesus forewarned us in John

15:18-20 that they would. "If the world hates you, ye know that it hated me before it hated you. If ye were of the world, the world would love his own: but because ye are not of the world, but I have chosen you out of the world, therefore the world hateth you. Remember the word that I said unto you, The servant is not greater than his lord. If they have persecuted me, they will also persecute you". However, GOD showed me that when persecution comes from the brethren, it is demonic. When we become accusers of our brothers and sisters in Christ, we join forces with Satan himself who is described in Revelations 12:10 as "the accuser of our brethren" accusing them day and night." Nevertheless, GOD uses persecution to test you and to prove what is in your heart. Can you love the person who wronged you? Can you forgive those who are fighting against you? Persecution is significant in the life of every believer because it identifies you with Christ. Paul said in Romans 8:17, "If so be that we suffer with him, that we may be also glorified together." Jesus suffered much persecution during His time here on earth. It was because He was the light of the world and darkness could not comprehend it. Therefore, those who opposed Jesus tried everything to destroy Him.

Persecution is only a sign that the life you live is godly. It is proof that you are a threat to the enemy and that Satan himself desires to stop the things of GOD in your life. The beauty of it is that there are promises that come along with persecution. Matthew 5:10 declares, "Blessed are they which are persecuted for righteousness' sake: for theirs is the kingdom of heaven." Not only that, but there is also a grace that covers you in your times of persecution. In 2 Corinthians Chapter 12,

Paul began to seek GOD concerning a thorn in his flesh. In return, GOD answered Paul by saying, "My grace is sufficient for thee: for my strength is made perfect in weakness". It was then that Paul got the revelation that even in suffering, persecution and affliction, GOD's presence and power are very present. Paul made the statement, "Most gladly therefore will I rather glory in my infirmities, that the power of Christ may rest upon me. Therefore I take pleasure in infirmities, in reproaches, in necessities, in persecutions, in distresses for Christ's sake: for when I am weak, then am I strong" (2 Corinthians 12: 9-10). Paul was inarguably saying that because he knew that his sufferings were for Christ's sake, he was able to find a reason to rejoice and find pleasure in his weaknesses. Take note that it is when you are weak within yourself, that you are strong in the Lord. We are commanded in Ephesians 6:10, "Finally, my brethren, be strong in the Lord, and in the power of his might".

The moment you step out to do anything for the Kingdom of GOD, expect resistance. In Acts Chapter 5, the Bible states that the apostles were given the power to do many miraculous signs and wonders among the people. Because of this, more and more people believed in the Lord and were added to the group of believers (Acts 5:14). However, the Sadducees became jealous, and the apostles were brought before the high priest. The high priest demanded that the apostles not use the name of Jesus. Peter and the apostles, however, boldly answered, "We must obey GOD and not man" (Acts 5:29). When the listening council heard this, they began plotting ways to kill the apostles. In other words, when you step out to start your ministry or follow a vision that GOD has given you, do not expect everyone to be on board with you. There will be people assigned by the enemy to stop what GOD is doing in your life. You will know the magnitude of your assignment and the level that you are on based on the level of the person sent by Satan to attack you. Here is what I am saying... When Jesus fasted for 40 days and 40 nights in the wilderness in Matthew Chapter 4, lower level demons did not show up to test Jesus. It was Satan himself that presented himself to tempt Christ. However, we can stand on the scripture in Isaiah 54:17 that declares, "No weapon that is formed against thee shall prosper; and every tongue that shall rise against thee in judgment thou shalt condemn." The scripture never said that the weapon would not be formed. However, it does make it clear that it would not prosper. And every tongue that rises against you in judgment, you shall condemn. The mere fact that GOD is blessing and moving in what you have set out to do for GOD, is what is going to cause the tongues to be condemned. There will be a spirit of conviction that comes on those who spoke against the moving of GOD in your life. Therefore, be confident that GOD is leading, guiding and instructing you and move in the boldness that Peter and the disciples moved in as they were fulfilling their God-given assignment. What is significant in Acts chapter 5 is that as the Sadducees and councilmen were planning ways to kill the apostles, there was a Pharisee in the crowd by the name of Gamaliel. Gamaliel stood up for the apostles and warned the councilmen to be very careful of what they were planning to do to the apostles. He stated in Acts 5:38-39 (ERV), "Stay away from these men. Leave them alone. If their plan is something they thought up, it will fail. But if it is from GOD, you will not be able to stop them. You might even be fighting against GOD himself." When people come against your God-given ministry, visions and ideas, they are not fighting against you. The scripture makes it clear that they are fighting against GOD himself. Who can stand against such a powerful GOD? Jesus told Saul on his way to Damascus to persecute the saints, "It is hard for thee to kick against the pricks" (Acts 9:5). A scripture comes to mind in Romans 8:30-31, "Moreover whom he did predestinate, them he also called: and whom he called, them he also justified: and whom he justified, them he also glorified. What shall we then say to these things? If God be for us, who can be against us?". My question to you is, if GOD be for you, who can be against you?

Rejection

In 2016, I wrote a book entitled "The Power of Rejection". In that book, GOD gave me the revelation that rejection is not only critical in the life of believers, but it is also necessary. When you have a call and a mandate from GOD on your life, rejection will come to push you into the place where GOD is preparing to take you. GOD uses rejection to keep you out of certain areas and situations that are not in His will for your life. Rejection also steers you away from those who have fulfilled their purpose and assignment in your life and even those who are sent by Satan to hinder and distract you on your journey towards destiny. When there is a sure fire anointing on your life, you will not be able to fit in, click up or hang out with everyone. The scripture in 2 Corinthians 6:17 says, "Come out from among them and be ye separate". A true sign of a leader is that he/she will not be able to fit in with the people they are trying to lead. Be a leader and stand out, even if it causes you to be rejected.

Rejection also reveals the hearts of men. People reject those who they no longer have the capacity for. There are just some individuals who will not be able to handle your greatness and success in GOD. They do not have the capacity or the ability to help push you into your destiny. They are not going where you are going. So in essence, to separate the two, GOD sends rejection. It is not a sign that something is wrong with you or that you are the problem, it is a sign that your destiny is calling you out by your name and it is time to get moving. "For all creation is waiting eagerly for that future day when God will reveal who his children really are" Romans 8:19 (NLT). Allow the rejection you have faced and will face to empower you.

CHAPTER 6:

"Ye Shall Receive Power"

I have preached my most powerful sermons under the unction, influence and consumption of the Holy Ghost. Within my ministry, I have seen people healed, filled and delivered through the powerful name of Jesus Christ. In order to experience the supernatural power of GOD on your life and in your ministry, there are a few elements that have to be present. You must first believe on Jesus and be saved. Following your salvation, you must be filled with the Holy Ghost and you must have faith in the powerful name of Jesus Christ and that name alone. GOD dropped a profound revelation in my spirit. He said, "The Holy Ghost comes upon you to produce power so that you may be a "witness" unto others. However, the name of Jesus produces the manifestation of signs, miracles and wonders so that those who "witness" it can become believers." The two work hand in hand.

Mark 16:17-18 says, "And these SIGNS shall follow them that BELIEVE; IN MY NAME shall they cast out devils; they shall speak with new tongues; they shall take up serpents; and if they drink any deadly thing, it shall not hurt them; they shall lay hands on the sick, and they shall recover." Did you catch the order of that scripture? Following your belief, comes a power within you to use the name of Jesus, causing signs of the miraculous to take place.

GOD highly exalted Jesus and gave Him a name that is above every name. At the name of Jesus, every knee should bow and every tongue confess that Christ is Lord. Jesus' name has given us unlimited power in many areas of our lives. Through His name, we have been given our identity as Christians. Acts 11:26, "And the disciples were called Christians first in Antioch."

As Christians, we now have the ability through the name of Jesus to access GOD. Jesus said in John 16:23-24 (NLT), "I tell you the truth, you will ask the Father directly, and he will grant your request because you use my name. You haven't done this before. Ask, using my name, and you will receive, and you will have abundant joy." The same power that was available when Jesus was on earth is now the exact same power you have when you use the name of Jesus. For example, we no longer have to press through the crowd to touch the hem of Jesus' garment to receive our healing (Matthew 9:20). We can now declare our healing in the name of Jesus, and that name delivers healing right to your front door. Not only that, but also the name of Jesus is our refuge and our safe place. Proverbs 18:10 declares, "The name of the Lord is a strong tower: the righteous runneth into it, and is safe." There is protection and safety in Jesus' name.

The first sign that Jesus said would follow those who believe, in Mark 16:17, would be that in His name, we have the ability and authority to cast out devils. This lets us know that as believers, there is a matchless power in the name of Jesus. The name of Jesus brings deliverance from the oppression of demonic spirits. In that name, we have been given authority, dominion and power. Luke 10:19 affirms, "Behold, I give unto you power to tread on serpents and scorpions, and over all the power of the enemy: and nothing shall by any means hurt you." Demons recognize the authority of Jesus and understand the power that has been given to His name. In Acts Chapter 16, there was a young girl, possessed by a spirit of divination, that followed Paul around saying, "These men are the servants of the most high GOD, which show us the way of salvation." The Bible indicates that Paul became so sore grieved that he turned and said to the spirit, "I command thee in the name of Jesus Christ to come out of her". Within that moment, the spirit came out of the girl. Examine this... Paul addressed the spirit, and not the girl. The Bible explains in Ephesians 6:12 that our battle is not against flesh and blood (people), but our battle is against principalities, powers, rulers of darkness of this world and spiritual wickedness in high places. Spirits use, embody and possess humans in order to carry out the works of evil and darkness. However, in the name of Jesus, we have been given power to cast the devil out.

It is in the name of Jesus that the lame walk, the deaf hear, the blind see, the lepers are cleansed, the sick are healed, the bound go free and sinners are saved. Use the authority you have been given by GOD through the powerful name of Jesus Christ. In Acts Chapter 3, Peter and John were headed together into the temple for prayer, when a man who had been lame since birth asked them for money. The Bible says in verse 6 that Peter spoke a profound statement to the man. He said unto him, "Silver and gold have I none; but such as I have give I thee: In the name of Jesus Christ of Nazareth rise up and walk." It was when Peter used the name of Jesus that the man's body began to receive strength and he stood up and walked into the temple with them praising GOD. Could it be that somebody is waiting on you to have enough faith to grab them by the hand and say, "In the name of Jesus, be healed, be delivered, be set free, walk, live, be happy..." As a baptized, Holy Ghost filled believer, use the authority and power given unto you through the powerful name of Jesus.

As believers, we lack in areas of our lives because we do not understand the true power that we have on the inside of us. Did you know that the same Spirit that raised Jesus from the dead lives on the inside of you (Romans 8:11)? There is reviving power flowing through your veins. This means, you have resurrecting power in you to speak to a dead thing and it has to live again, Ezekiel. In Ezekiel 37, Ezekiel was placed in a valley of dry bones. While in that valley, the LORD told Ezekiel to prophesy to the bones. When Ezekiel began to prophesy to the bones, there was a noise and a shaking and the bones came together. GOD then told Ezekiel to prophesy again. This time, He commanded Ezekiel to prophecy to the four winds. The winds in this passage of scripture are representative of the Spirit of GOD and the ruach of GOD, translated, the breath of GOD. As Ezekiel prophesied to the four winds, breath came into the bodies and they lived. It is quite interesting that it was not until after the bodies had been filled with the breath of GOD that they began to live. Meaning, you will not experience the fullness of life until you have God's Spirit living on the inside of you. The key to this whole scripture is the fact that Ezekiel prophesied and spoke over the bones, and that is when the elements began to shift. What am I saying? As a believer, you have the power to speak to the situations in your life and cause things to shift and change. The first instruction Jesus gave in Mark 11:22 (NIV) was, "Have faith in GOD". He followed that statement by then saying, "If anyone says to this mountain, 'Go, throw yourself into the sea,' and does not doubt in their heart but believes that what they say will happen, it will be done for them." The key to having what you say is to not doubt, but to have faith in GOD. When you use the powerful name of Jesus, then you can speak your declarations with boldness, being confident that it will happen. In Joshua Chapter 10 verse 12, the Bible states that Joshua spoke to the Lord and in the sight of Israel, Joshua commanded the sun to stand still. For an entire day, the sun stood still. The Bible records, "And there was no day like that before it or after it, that the Lord hearkened unto the voice of a man". By faith, Joshua spoke and it happened. Elijah, a prophet of GOD, demonstrated these same principles in 1 Kings 17 verse 1 when he declared, "As surely as the Lord, the God of Israel lives, the God I serve, there will be no dew or rain during the next few years until I give the word". According to the words he spoke, there was no rain for over a period of three years. The truth is, we have the power on the inside of us to shift economics, climates and atmospheres. You have the power within you to dominate areas and overtake regions by the power of the Holy Ghost. Matthew 18:18 (NIV) declares, "Whatever you bind on earth will be bound in heaven, and whatever you loose on earth will be loosed in heaven." Your faith releases a power in and through the words that you speak.

Job 22:28 declares, "Thou shalt also decree a thing, and it shall be established unto thee". In essence, this scripture is saying, you shall command a thing and it shall come forth. "Death and life are in the power of the tongue: and they that love it shall eat the fruit thereof" (Proverbs 18:21). The fruit that produces in your life is a direct result of the things you have spoken. There is power in the words that you speak. If there is a healing that you need, decree over your life that by

Jesus' stripes you are healed (Isaiah 53:5). If you are believing GOD for a financial breakthrough, decree, all of my needs are supplied according to GOD's riches in glory (Philippians 4:19). If you are saved and you are believing for your children to be saved, decree that no good thing will GOD withhold from them that walk upright (Psalm 84:11). As you decree declarations over your life and over the lives of those that are connected to you, speak GOD's Word, believe by faith in the name of Jesus, and watch it come to pass. You have unlimited power. Whenever you speak the Word of GOD, it becomes a shield against the darts of the enemy and it becomes a driving force in the supernatural things of GOD.

Another area in your life that GOD wants you to know that you have power in is to be a witness through the empowerment of His Spirit. Acts 1:8

"But ye shall receive power, after that the Holy Ghost is come upon you: and ye shall be witnesses unto me both in Jerusalem, and in all Judaea, and in Samaria, and unto the uttermost part of the earth." The anointing of the Holy Ghost on your life is necessary to draw others unto to Christ and to destroy yokes. All throughout the book of Acts, you will find where the apostles were enabled by the Spirit of GOD to speak boldly the word of GOD and in turn, this helped to add souls to the church daily. GOD wants to empower you to be light in dark places. He needs someone that He can fill with His Spirit that will not be afraid to unlock hell's gates and set those that are bound, free. Isaiah 61:1-3 declares, " The Spirit of the Lord God is upon me; because the Lord hath anointed me to preach good tidings unto the meek; he hath sent me to bind up the brokenhearted, to proclaim liberty to the captives, and the opening of the prison to them that are bound; To proclaim the acceptable year of the Lord, and the day of vengeance of our God; to comfort all that mourn; To appoint unto them that mourn in Zion, to give unto them beauty for ashes, the oil of joy for mourning, the garment of praise for the spirit of heaviness; that they might be called trees of righteousness, the planting of the Lord, that he might be glorified." When the Spirit of the Lord comes upon you, whether you are in a pulpit or in the grocery store, you are empowered to announce freedom in Christ Jesus to them that are bound. For GOD has not given us a spirit of fear, but of POWER.

I once heard a profound prophet say, "No gift is better, just different". Meaning, just because I am empowered to prophesy one way and you are empowered to prophesy another way, it does not make my gift any better than yours, or your gift any better than mine. It just makes the gift different in the form of administration. However, in contrast, there are some gifts that carry a heavier weight of glory and anointing on them than others. This is due to that particular individual's willingness to allow the Holy Spirit to rest, rule, abide, operate, correct and control their lives. Never forget, holiness is key to extreme power. Along with holiness, there are other elements that release dunamis power in your life. Elements such as prayer and fasting unlock supernatural doors that release supernatural power. In Mark Chapter 9, an unnamed man brought his son, who was possessed by a deaf and dumb spirit, to the disciples to cast the spirit out. However, the disciples were unable to cast the devil out of the boy. The man then took his son to Jesus. Jesus cast the spirit out of the boy and commanded it to never return again. When the disciples were alone with Jesus they asked, "Why weren't we able to cast the spirit out?" Jesus said unto them in verse 29, "This kind can come forth by nothing, but by prayer and fasting". Your prayer life and a lifestyle that includes continual fasting, unleashes the power of GOD against vile demonic spirits. It also opens up a gateway that you may move and operate in supernatural power and demonstrations.

On one occasion in Mark Chapter 9, the 12 disciples had a discussion where they disputed among themselves who should be considered the greatest among them. Jesus sat them down and explained to the disciples in verse 35, "If any man desires to be first, the same shall be last of all, and servant of all." The Bible says in Matthew 20:28 (NIV), "...the Son of man did not come to be served, but to serve..." There is a requirement to being first in the Kingdom of GOD. The requirement is to make yourself last and become a servant. In essence, this crucifies your flesh and desires, and allows you to be as humble as Jesus was. Servitude positions you in a place where GOD can extend His power unto you and make you great. Understand this...there is no popularity in being a servant. The servant is most often overlooked and counted out. You will not be recognized when you are a servant. In contrast, however, servitude grants you a magnitude of power. Power over Popularity! This is why the scripture says in Matthew 20:16, "The last shall be first, and the first last: for many be called, but few chosen". What GOD is saying to us is, if you make yourself last, He can make you first. If you humble yourself, He can exalt you. I would rather GOD exalt me than man. Due to the unreliability of man's feelings and opinions, which can change within an instance, one day man will shout, "Hosanna, Hosanna" and the next day, "Crucify Him". Nevertheless, there is a power that lies in your ability to walk in humility. Humble yourself and commit yourself to being least among them by being a servant to all of them. In return, GOD says, "I will exalt you and empower you, and I will make your name great".

CHAPTER 7:

"Wake Up"

Once during a service, as I was ministering, the LORD spoke through me and said that the church was asleep. One definition of the word sleep is, "to be dormant". Another term for dormant is, "inactive". What GOD was ultimately saying was, the church is inactively dormant. There are gifts on the inside of you that are inactive and untapped. There are powerful individuals sitting within a church but are not being actively used or activated. In order to be active, you must be engaged. Your gift must be exercised. You will never know what is on the inside of a closed box until you open it. This book was written with the purpose to wake up and unlock the power on the inside of you. If you are a believer, then in the name of Jesus, I speak to the gift on the inside of you, Wake Up! Arise, o sleeper! Arise out of your slumber! There were many studies done that proved that if a person gets too much sleep, it causes various health issues which can lead to organ failure and even death. For some of you reading this book, you have been sleep too long. Adversely, this has caused you to feel that what was once on the inside of you is now dead and gone. It is interesting that the word "wake" is used to describe the viewing of a dead body. Therefore, the purpose of this book is to "wake" UP what you thought had died. GOD said, "It never left, and it is not dead. It is just asleep". I come in the name of Jesus and I call forth those gifts within you and command them to Wake Up! In the name of Jesus, word of wisdom, wake up! Word of knowledge, wake up! Faith, wake up! Gifts of healing, wake up! Working of miracles, wake up! Gift of prophecy, wake up! Discerning of spirits, wake up! Divers kinds of tongues, wake up! Interpretation of tongues, wake up! The Bible says in 1 Corinthians 12:7-11, "But the manifestation of the Spirit is given to every man to profit withal. For to one is given by the Spirit the word of wisdom; to another the word of knowledge by the same Spirit; To another faith by the same Spirit; to another the gifts of healing by the same Spirit; To another the working of miracles; to another prophecy; to another discerning of spirits; to another divers kinds of tongues; to another the interpretation of tongues: But all these worketh that one and the selfsame Spirit, dividing to every man severally as he will." If you are ready to go to the next level in GOD, wake up! Talents and ideas, wake up! Books and songs, wake up! Kingdom businesses and church blueprints, wake up! Dreams and visions, wake up! Pastors, Ministers, Evangelists, psalmists, book writers, worship leaders, songwriters and others that are destined to do great things for the

Kingdom of GOD, wake up! GOD is calling you by your name! He is ready to anoint you with fresh fire. Put popularity aside and receive Holy Ghost power. The world is waiting on you. Your family needs you. Your community is depending on you. I believe right now by the power of GOD that is vested in me, you can ask GOD right where you are to fill you with the Holy Ghost and anoint you afresh, and He will do it. GOD is ready to shake the gates of hell and take it by storm, and He wants to use you to do it. Are you ready? Do you want it? Receive it NOW in the name of Jesus.

"...These that have turned the world upside down..."

Acts 17:6

"POWER OVER POPULARITY"

www.ayannahwilliamsministries.com

AYANNAH WILLIAMS MINISTRIES

Be sure to visit online @

www.ayannahwilliamsministries.com

Sermon Clips · Speaking Engagements Schedule ·

Order Books · Prayer Requests... and more!

facebook.com/MinisterAyannahWilliams

@MinisterAyannah

@Ayannah_Williams

www.ingramcontent.com/pod-product-compliance
Lightning Source LLC
Chambersburg PA
CBHW062020040426
42447CB00010B/2076